Trapped in the Lies
of Your Truth

Trapped in the Lies of Your Truth

Finding yourself through the struggles of life by facing your internal issues masked with external deception

Destiny U. Barrett

Book Design & Production
Columbus Publishing Lab
www.ColumbusPublishingLab.com

Paperback ISBN: 978-1-63337-065-4
E-book ISBN: 978-1-63337-068-5

LCCN: 2015954889

Printed in the United States of America
1 3 5 7 9 10 8 6 4 2

Inspired by Sarah Jakes and the singer Monica

Introduction

IN OCTOBER OF 2007 I began to write this book. I pre ti-
tled it *Life is What You Make It*. Through life's experiences I
realized that my life was what I made it. During this time in
my life, I was living fast, making fast money, driving fast cars
in and out of town, and would go from having it all down to
having nothing at all. But one thing was for sure – I always
managed to keep my head above water and would always find
a way to bounce back. But through my finding I found out that
easy come, easy go.

As I began to write my life's story, there came a time
when I could not write any more, and life's detours did not
provide me a chance to sit down and focus. Several events have

taken place between then and now. One of these events brought me to my knees and forced me to make a promise to God that I had no choice but to keep. That promise was, "Lord, if you get me out of this situation, I will give you my life and never turn back." Oh, did he hold me to that. From that point on, my life was never the same.

In May of 2014, I enrolled in online classes for human services and child developmental psychology. I went through my first eight weeks and lost my focus. During June of 2014, I lost my job of six years. At this point, I was overwhelmed between school, work and other things going on in my life. I was never the type to just lay down and die. I immediately went into survival mode, but this time, the difference was that I knew Jesus. Me knowing Jesus didn't stop the hurt, didn't stop the tears, and didn't stop the questions, but it gave me peace and security that if I would only believe, trust and put my faith in God, he would sustain me.

I had a house with $900 rent, a car with a near $500 payment, house bills and a 14-year-old daughter that I was raising alone. So I dropped my online courses for six months to get myself on track and regain my focus. When I lost my job, I still had $600 coming in every two weeks through a side job I had as a home health aide, and I also received unemployment. In between, I began to work as a hair stylist in a studio loft where

Trapped in the Lies of Your Truth

I had very few clients and business was up and down. As I was driving to work one day, God began to speak to me. He said, "You will go through a dry place, but I will sustain you." I instantly began to thank God because I could only imagine what I was about to experience.

My side job ended. There was no more $600 every two weeks, my unemployment ran out after six months, and my $900 rent was now $1,100. I was truly set up on a faith walk. In December of 2014 I picked my online classes back up. I went through the first week and could not go any further. At that point, I was so confused, overwhelmed and ready to give up. So I began to pray and ask God to order my steps. I had a dilemma with whether or not to stay or drop out of school. Between school and trying to build my clientele, it was stressing me out – not to mention personal issues that were hurting my heart. I went to my parents and asked them what I should do because I was lost and confused. Of course, they discussed this with me, but at the end of our conversation, they told me I would need to go to God, as he can only give you the direction that he wants you to go. So that is just what I did. I got my answer clear as day. While walking around my kitchen cooking, cleaning, singing and praying, God spoke these words to me.

Matthew 9:17

*"Neither do men put old wine into new wineskins
otherwise they will break and the wine runs out and
the wineskins perish. But those who put new wine
into new wineskins both are preserved together."*

God said, "You are so filled up with mess that it has become toxic, and it will reject anything new you try to put in. You have to release, and your release will come through your writing. Through your writing will birth your purpose."

So before I could pursue a degree and be filled up with more credentials, I had to release the issues of my heart that had become toxic and prevented me from operating in purpose and using my gifts. So pretty much once I catch up, he will give me more. All that week and the week before I had been listening to James Fortune's "Empty Me" over and over. God was ministering and preparing my spirit to receive his direction.

Luke 12:48

"To whomever much is given much will be required."

I broke this series of my story down into five letters just to open up, catch your attention and lay down a foundation before entering in on a deeper level.

Trapped in the Lies of Your Truth

I began this series at the turning point of my life because this is when God began to rebirth my purpose. I hope to touch someone's heart, trigger a change, and most of all influence someone to become a believer in Christ, because he definitely lives.

Letter 1:
Uncovering the Truth

ALL MY LIFE, I hid my true feelings of the way I felt about myself. No one would ever know because of the way I carried on, and my presentation was so convincing. Everyone I interacted with thought I was so thorough, but what they did not know and could not see was a girl who was hurt, lost, confused and insecure. A girl who hated who she was and looked at people that she wished she could be or look like. A girl who felt like every man she had put other women above her. There were so many more undercover feelings that led to thoughts like, "Why everybody but me?" A girl who would tell all kinds of lies to make herself relevant in the society she was living in. Everyone thought I was this strong woman with no worries and all the answers, but they had no idea what I went through behind closed doors. They had no idea of the hurt and pain I felt, or the tears I cried when it was just me alone by myself. I became so immune to these feelings that building walls became natural. Even if something bothered me, I would tell myself that I didn't care to the point that I really wouldn't. Well, at least I thought I didn't. What I was doing was building barriers and suppressing internal issues that would eventually surface.

Proverbs 4:23

"Above all else, guard your heart for it determines the course of your life." (New Living Translation)

"Keep your heart with all diligence; for out of it flows the issues of life." (King James Version)

See, when I was living the fast life, it was easy to hide all of these things. I was able to cover it up with men, drugs, liquor, money, cars, clothing, and getaway trips out of town. But once you leave that lifestyle, you are forced to face it all. It's just you, your problems and God. Oh but yes, sometimes it feels like God is nowhere near, and whether you believe it or not, that's when he is the nearest and just waiting for you to call on him.

I choose to expose this issue because there are many women and young ladies that have or are currently experiencing/battling this same internal condition. To say the least, most females would not dare to admit or speak on it. I know I will get so many different responses from this regarding my character, and that's ok, it's to be expected. I am ok with that because I know who I am now! I understand that God made me so fearful and wonderful that the enemy had to try and destroy me before I figured that out. And oh, was the attack so real, direct and personal.

If you are reading this book and you are dealing with issues as such, you are not alone. These thoughts and feelings do not make you who you are, but they can break you if you do not acknowledge them and properly deal with them. The first person you have to be real with is yourself, and you must confess it unto the Lord.

So get by yourself, and confess those very things that you cannot utter to man (people) to God. "God I am this, I have done that, I don't want to be this way." Anything that has you in bondage, weighing you down, causing you to feel victimized or guilty, speak it out of your mouth. Then tell God, "I surrender it all to you. Take it, I don't want it." Don't allow the enemy to lie to you any longer, as it will be a continuous struggle until the enemy knows he can no longer use it against you. He will still try to creep up on you, so you have to stay prepared at all times – ready for war. The enemy is coming straight for your mind. Understand that you have power over any thought that comes to invade your mind. We choose what we think.

2 Corinthians 10:5
"We are destroying speculations and every lofty
thing raised up against the knowledge of God, and
we are taking every thought captive to the
obedience of Christ."

Philippians 4:8
"Finally, brothers and sisters, keep your thoughts
on whatever is right and deserves praise: things
that are true, honorable, fair, pure, acceptable, or
commendable." (Gods Word Translation)

As I look back and become more mature in my under-standing, I see that God allowed me to walk through many sea-sons of this and experience these feelings and thoughts so that I could effectively minister this book to you and help others in need. What you have to understand is that seasons do not last forever. At all times, you have to walk in the spirit and follow God's leading so that you will not get stuck walking in high boots during the summertime.

This letter was purposed to break up the grounds of internal lies covered up by external deception turned into truth. We will go deeper in the next series.

Letter 2:
Looking for Love

A CLOSE FAMILY FRIEND I considered my "cousin" would always make a statement calling me a "looking for love chick." Of course, I was extremely offended and went straight into defense mode. The person I was or the person I created could care less about a man, loving a man, and whoever or whatever else. It was fun while it lasted then on to the next – your loss not mine. I painted a picture as if I had no worries, and in my mind, I didn't. But deep down within there was a lost little girl who just wanted a man who would take her and love her, but rejection made me heartless. All the guys would say, "You are worse than a man." All the females would say, "You better watch out for her, she doesn't play fair." When a female would cross me,

I wouldn't be one who would want to fight, unless I had to defend myself. I would hit you where it hurt, keep it moving like it was nothing, and dare you to come for me.

I can still remember my first hurt from a boy. I was in the 7th grade and my boyfriend went behind me and started to date another girl. She would buy him tickets to our school's basketball games and pushed herself right up on him. Plus she was having sex and I wasn't. His sister had a sleepover for her birthday. We were friends, and she said that she wanted to invite me, but because the other girl was dating her brother she had to invite her. I remember sitting on my bed talking to him on the phone and he admitted that she was his new girlfriend. It felt like someone stabbed me in my heart. I can feel it now when I think about it. Of course, I was young, so I really had no true understanding of what was going on. I just knew I did not like it. That was my first hurt experience from a man that I considered myself "dating." And sure enough, it did not stop.

As I got older and began to come in tune with the spirit of God, I realized that men were my weakness and men were what the enemy was trying to use to destroy me. He used them to attempt to physically kill me, which did not work, so he had to attack me from within. He put a personal attack on my heart and my mind. Up until I found God, it was making me more bitter, resentful, hateful and heartless. It was starting to destroy me. Either my feelings were deeply involved and somewhere down the line rejection took place, or the guy was so attached to me that it turned me off. I was messed up, and I wanted whom I thought I loved, and not who loved me.

For years, I entangled myself with different men. Some were long-term relationships and some were short-term. Others were one or two time interactions. I created a tight bond with some of the men and we became close "friends." Our interactions depended on time and how we were feeling. Subconsciously, deep down I wanted one of the relationships to last forever.

This brings us back to "looking for love" in all the wrong places. One thing I admire about myself is that through all the bitterness and resentment that began to take place in my heart, I never adopted a bitter mindframe such as, "All men are the same" (because I know there're not), "Never trust a man" (not all men are to be trusted, but there are men who can be trusted), etc. I always had the ability to love again. Now, I may keep my guard way up, but I was always willing to open my heart. I'm not sure if this is a good or bad thing. In my opinion, it could be both.

What I came to realize is that no matter how much time you spend with someone, no matter how long you have been with someone, or to what extent you take the relationship, if it is not the man/woman that God designed for you, it will not last and there will be no real peace in it.

The purpose of this letter is to give my readers insight on the detrimental position a man can potentially have in your life, and how important it is to seek God before pursuing a relationship of any kind. In my opinion, men are all women's weakness in some form at some point in life. This short letter is just to break up grounds and encourage women to evaluate relationships and attachments. Look forward to the next series for more in-depth revelations.

The enemy is not so much worried about the
women. His aim is to destroy and corrupt our men
because women will attach themselves to men so
firmly that they will destroy themselves.
~T.D. Jakes

Letter 3:
You Are Your Own Worst Enemy

ONE DAY, WHILE IN prayer, God revealed to me the revelation that, "I am my own worst enemy." As Henry van Dyke stated, "Self is the only prison that can bind the soul." I have always taken responsibility for my actions, but I also took offenses to heart and felt I had to prove my point. My parents had a headquarters where they would have church before they got a building. There would be days when I would go down to the headquarters to get away by myself just to release, pray, sing and read. It was the only place I could go to free my mind with no filters. So this day, while I was praying, I began to speak the words, "Ok, God." I repeated these words, but I had no idea what I was saying, "Ok" to. As I proceeded in praying, I began to walk around and praise God. There was a very big full-body wall-to-wall mirror in the room. As I was walking toward the mirror with my eyes closed, I opened my eyes and jumped very hard. It appeared that someone was in the room with me, but I knew I was alone. I was so scared, but I laughed so hard when I realized it was "me" in the mirror.

Then God began to speak, "You are your own worst enemy. It's not the people, it's you."

And again, those words came back, "Ok, God. I get it!"

See, God will prepare your spirit before he speaks so that the word will be received. You are your own worst enemy. You control your "hurt," you control your "healing," you control "hate," you control your "love," you control your "bitterness," you control your "forgiveness," you control your "procrastination," and you control your "prosperity." God never promised that we would not experience the malfunctions of this world, but he did promise a way out and provided us with a way to deal with hurt, anger, bitterness, etc. Many people had wronged me. Some were more effective than others, while some just bounced off of me as if they never existed. What I wasn't realizing was that I was creating barriers in my heart, which were making it hard for God's word to fall on good grounds.

Trapped in the Lies of Your Truth

Proverbs 16:11
"Good sense makes one slow to anger,
and it is his glory to overlook an offense."

Ecclesiastes 7:21-22
"Do not take to heart all the things that people say,
lest you hear your servant cursing you.
For you know in your heart that many times
you yourself have cursed others."

One of my favorite sayings is, "If they sin with you, they will sin against you." It comes with the territory when you are living a lifestyle outside of the will of God. Once I processed this understanding, I was able to do some self-evaluation. Anytime I was offended by someone's action or words and began to form my opinion and defense, I resorted back to myself. I evaluated what was going on inside of me. What am I lacking that I am so easily offended and able to hold a grudge?

Holding a grudge was one valuable lesson that I have learned. I was an extreme grudge holder. I could hold a grudge for so long I forgot why I was even mad, I just knew I didn't deal with you. To me, nothing was petty. The way I saw it was: if you can do something so small and petty, then I can only imagine the big things you are capable of doing, and you are not to be trusted. If I felt violated or crossed in any way, I had no interaction with you, especially if we were considered friends.

I am a thinker – at times, I can think a little too long, hard and deep. I can admit that because of this, at times, I created deeper issues than what should have been. The reason being, all of the mess I took in was saturated and compressed and would seep out periodically. It was not until I held a grudge with a very close person in my life up until the day before he passed away that it clicked within me that I could no longer operate in this state of being. If I had not gone to the hospital the day before my friend passed and let go of the grudge, I would not know how to live with myself. In the next series, I will elaborate more in-depth on this situation.

The purpose of this letter is to encourage my readers to eliminate everyone but self. Search within and examine your heart. One thing I have realized is that a person can quickly see someone else's faults or flaws, but they can hardly see, accept or even acknowledge their own.

Matthew 7:3 (English Standard Version)
"Why do you see the speck that is in your brother's
eye, but do not notice the log that is in your own eye."
(let that marinate)

Trapped in the Lies of Your Truth

You will find that there are some situations you have found offensive that are not the fault of that person, but a previous hurt that has not been dealt with lingering around in your heart. Anything that looks like that hurt causes it to rise up, and you respond from a bitter heart caused by a past hurt. There are other situations that you may just need to flat out let go of and forgive. What does it profit you to continue holding on and responding to it?

Proverbs 4:23
"Above all else, guard your heart;
for out of it flows the issues of life."

Letter 4:
A Contingent Marriage

1 Corinthians 13:9-10
"For we know in part and we prophesy in part,
but when completeness comes, part will disappear."

We pray, God answers. We hear, "Yes," and we ignore "But not now." We ignore "Yes," but not him/her. We hear what we want and then put a Jesus stamp on our own stuff. We move in our own understanding and can't understand why it falls apart. It's because we did not wait on the Lord.

In June of 2010 I convinced myself that God gave me the ok to marry my ex-husband. I came up with all kinds of reasons as to how I knew it was God that put us together. Although God did have a plan, I put my own twist to it. But the truth was that I was looking for love in all the wrong places. My heart desired a husband so badly that I settled for the first man at that time who was willing to marry me. It felt good because I had someone I could call my own. I didn't care what the situation looked like because he was mine. My focus was based on the hope of what could be or what I wanted it to be. What I ignored was the fact that he had been in prison for the past ten years, and once he was released, it would be a gamble on the direction he would take in life. I could not afford to gamble with my life. Nearly two years later, our marriage began to fall apart. The truth to it all is, we both married each other for selfish reasons, and it was easy to do because we had history going back from before he went to prison.

So, as time progressed, the relationship was going up and down. Being in the public society provided me with a chance to grow as a woman and mature to different levels in many areas of life. Versus him, who had been locked in prison for so long that he did not have the chance to grow and experience relationships and life on the same level to fully mature as an adult. However, that did not take away from who he was overall, but it caused severe miscommunication. He would think from a one-track mind, which would cause him to handle situations the only way he knew how – the way he would have handled

Destiny U. Barrett

them ten years ago before he went to prison. This was because his mind would not register situations past the typical cause for the issue at hand. My issue was that I was slow to mature in the area of handling my emotions. I would act on what I felt if it touched my pride, and made some very immature decisions. These two characteristics definitely did not mix and caused a huge fire that led to divorce.

My ex-husband and I have history. It was not all good but not all bad. There was a situation as teenagers and young adults we faced that caused me to part ways from him back then. He was one of the first men to tamper with my feelings and cause me to create walls at an early age. He made a child with another woman and then moved in with her. In my mind, he chose her, but yet he still wanted me around. I was so hurt, but my lifestyle would not permit me to show it. The hurt I felt caused me to shut down completely. I would act as if he did not exist when I saw him. Although we would still interact from time to time, I never let my guard down. A couple years later, he went to prison.

Years passed before we reconnected. But once we did, within one year we were married. Different sorts of issues would begin to arise that would trigger my weaknesses and cause me to begin building walls all over again. I started going through changes. I became lonely, and I felt like I wanted to be touched. I started to feel as if another woman ultimately had control over my husband's feelings because of their children, which was something I refused to compete with.

Men at my workplace and random men I would run into would attempt to pursue me. In my mind, no matter what I was feeling or what I was going through, I was someone's wife, and there was nothing that would make me act on those feelings. I had excellent examples of what marriage looked like, and in my words, marriage is a completely different part of the game and not to be played with. I always say that once you marry, you no longer have to answer to your boyfriend or girlfriend, you have to answer to God, whom you committed vows before.

So, as time went by, I found myself entertaining conversations with other men, and issues continued to arise with my husband and me. One thing that I vowed to myself was that if I had no respect for anyone, I would maintain a respect for God and the vows I took before him, and I would never have sex with anyone. It actually was never a desire or a thought that crossed my mind because ultimately I loved my husband and had way more respect for myself than to go that route. Also, thinking back on the lifestyle I lived prior to giving my life to God, I just refuse to give a man that kind of power over me.

I began to realize that my husband and I were ruining a friendship. Not only that, but we had a child in-between us. I felt it was best for us to undo the mess we created, rebuild a friendship and get closer to God on an individual basis, so that when he was released from prison, if I was still what he wanted, and it was God's will, we could remarry the right way.

So I filed for an annulment. He was not happy about it at all! From there, the relationship spiraled downhill. Losing or leaving him was never my intention. I assured him that nothing would change but our title. I was not saying that I did not want to be with him, I was just saying I needed to get myself together so that I could be the wife God designed me to be, and make sure this is where we were supposed to be. We had rushed into this marriage prematurely, and it was damaging our friendship and our daughter was being affected by it. He could not see past the fact, that in his mind, I was saying that I did not want to be with him. He totally disregarded the point of everything that I was saying. With a one-track mind, he felt that the only time a woman wants to leave a man is when there is another man involved. As I stated, that is only true when a woman has no morals and God and self are not top priority. Furthermore, I was not leaving, I just felt it was best that we not proceed on in a marriage and destroy our relationship to the point of no return.

Then, in my eyes, he did the ultimate. My husband reached back out to the mother of one of his children in efforts to get my attention, or so he said. He definitely got my attention, just not the way he expected to get it. Due to the history behind this whole ordeal, it shut me all the way down. Every hope I had was gone. This is an example of him not being able to mature in certain areas of relationships. This is the game we used to play in our early to mid 20s. In time, we mature from that place through experience because we gain a proper understanding that it only causes more drama, and we gain a different level of respect for soft spots in relationships. That was a very sensitive spot in our relationship, so to me, he took the gloves off and gave the enemy ammunition.

I began to open up to a guy that I had no intentions of interacting with as a resort to how I was feeling. However, I maintained my level of respect due to the fact that I was still legally married, and regardless of what he had done, I still had to maintain self-respect. No one could run back and tell my husband anything. No one knew the guy, and we had no mutual friends besides the ones we met at our workplace. We came from two completely different worlds. But oh, did this start a whole other chapter in my life. I won't get into that in this series, so you will have to follow me on my journey, and I promise to be as transparent as God allows me to be. You will be blessed to know that you are not alone and that God gives his hardest battles to his strongest people.

The purpose of me briefly sharing this story is to relate

with women who are going through, or have been through, a similar situation. A woman longs for companionship, and we often settle for less than what God has in store for us by becoming anxious or not knowing how to wait on the Lord. We put ourselves in situations that we could have prevented, and we play the victim when it spirals out of control. God will give you warning before going into a situation that is not designed for you. He will give you direction to remove yourself. When we fail to be obedient, he will allow a situation to take place that will force us to move and cause us not to ever be able to return to it in peace unless it is his will and his timing. We cannot make anything work that is not in God's will.

Today, as I am writing this letter, I am single. I currently have a soul tie to my ex-husband that I am positioning myself for God to take care of. Right now, as I am writing this letter, there is a moving in my heart and chills running through my body that lets me know that soul tie needs to be broken. To be honest, if certain things were not going on in my life at that time, I would probably still be married to him. At times, I feel like I gave my family away. He is currently interacting with another female, and we all know our nonchalant attitude when we are being pacified. There are many angles and levels to that, and I learned the hard way that it is not my duty to expose or even give attention to it. The enemy will slowly destroy you by putting something or someone in your life to block the real issues that need to be addressed. You will think that you are over something that you're not. When the enemy knows your weaknesses, he will use them against you every chance he gets until it no longer affects you, and then he can't use it any more. He used my ex-husband to the fullest. He was so angry, hurt and so many more mixed emotions. In addition, he never accepted his part in our downfall – he would do all types of things just to make me feel what he was feeling. That began to cause more hatred inside of me until I realized what it was. Then we brought other people into our mess without truly cleansing our heart from each other. Those people were distractions and the enemy's way of keeping us in bondage. Because once something goes wrong, it's double trouble. Now, not only are we faced with suppressed feelings and issues that were lying dormant between us, we now have to deal with the people we connected ourselves to in order to cover up how we were really feeling, which created another soul tie. When another person comes along in a time that you are in an unstable, emotional, hurt and lonely place, it is easy to attach yourself to that person when they show concern. At that time, it's what you need, so you jump in head first with no regard for the additional chaos you are creating.

What God has for you is for you, and what God has for me

is for me. In order to receive what he has, there is a humbling that has to take place, and I have to let go of the past. Before you receive the real thing, sometimes the enemy will send the imitation, and this is when you see if you have a real connection with God to discern the difference. It will feel so right, and once you get in too deep, the mask comes off. They are like wolves in sheep's clothing. God places people in our lives for a reason, whether it's for a season or a lifetime. When the purpose is fulfilled, he will remove them or continue to peacefully build. We pervert the cause by holding on after the reason is fulfilled or the season has passed by making it more than what it was intended to be. I pray that God brings me to a place where the friendship between my ex-husband and myself is restored and we can effectively co-parent our daughter.

The purpose of this letter is to encourage women to wait on the Lord. He has the perfect man for you – one who does not require you to compete for a position, one you don't have to pressure to love you in any kind of way. My grandmother once told me, "Destiny, just focus on you. Establish your relationship with God and a man will recognize the light shining through you and want to be a part of it." These words stuck with me ever since she spoke them to me. These words were so profound because she had no idea what I was going through and it was right on time. Let that word settle in your heart. Love yourself first. When you truly love yourself you are clearly able to identify if someone else genuinely loves you. Would you intentionally inflict any hurt on yourself? A person who truly loves you wouldn't either.

Keys to peace:
- Recognize the issue
- Admit there is an issue
- Eliminate everyone but yourself to see where you went wrong
- Accept that it is what it is
- Lean on God for direction and follow his leading
- Wait on the Lord
- Let Go and let God

Philippians 4:7
"And the peace of God that surpasses all under-standing will guide your heart and mind."

Letter 5:
Twisted Identity

ONE THING ABOUT ME is that I was never a follower. Even while I was in the world I never wanted to hang out in groups. So if it was three or more people, I probably wasn't going. I was pretty quiet for the most part unless I was really comfortable around you. Most of the females I associated with were loud and rowdy so my quietness was often mistaken for weakness, but I was far from weak. I have always been the type to own up to my actions. I kept it real with whoever, whenever. I was a natural to the street life, and I adapted as soon as I hit the streets at sixteen. I got my first apartment when I was nineteen and my first car when I was twenty. I got them both on my own and have had my own ever since. Even if it was a struggle, I always managed to keep my head above water.

For seven years my life repeated a cycle. I would have everything I needed – job, car, house, money and extra things that weren't even a necessity. But I would lose it all. While in this time of my yearly downfall, I would always make sure I had money in my pocket, so the hustle was continuous. Sometimes I would be down bad, but you would not be able to tell by looking at me, and I made the struggle look good. Any way I could make money I was down and ready to get it, but I always maintained a level of respect for myself.

The worst part about being in this place is that you don't think with a clear mind. There were so many different thoughts going through my mind that I could not process one thought, which caused me to make premature decisions. This also caused me to subject myself to things and people I normally would not have. This state of being was very uncomfortable and downgrading for me because I was a person people viewed as being "bossy," so I could never allow them to see or know I was down bad. Out of pride, I jeopardized my life and freedom to get back to a place where I could uphold my image. I participated in many illegal activities and other things as well. I would not stay in that down place too long because my hustle instinct would kick into overdrive. I had built relationships with some of the major players in and outside of the city and they trusted me, so my connections were plenty.

As I reflect back on these times, God was providing me an opportunity to reach out to him so that he could clean up my life and cultivate the strong-willed, determined, trustworthy woman for his purpose for which he made me. But instead, I continued on in what I knew and the lifestyle I was comfortable with – the easy way out. To be honest, in the first couple years of experiencing this cycle, God was the furthest thing from my mind. I was in so deep that I did not have a conscience. I would stay aware of my surroundings and find a smarter way to do the wrong thing. I would seldom pray and had no intentions of changing my lifestyle, but God never stopped talking to me. He would speak through some of the craziest people. However, I could always identify his voice, even in my mess. I could have been in the dope house and a drug addict would randomly say something that would put my antennas straight up. Such as, "You know the graveyard is full of people who never fulfilled their purpose." Random people would say, "What are you doing? You don't belong out here." But they wouldn't even know me. I would always hear that I was different.

No matter what image you try to portray, you can never truly hide what and who you are. Your true identity will always stand out. That's why it is so important to know who you are. When the person you created begins to clash with the person

God designed you to be, you begin to fight for an identity. You have so many battling characteristics that you don't even know which ones are yours.

I adopted so many different personalities to adapt in environments where I did not belong. I endured so many emotional, mental and physical situations that the average female would not be able to stand through. I thank God for making me the woman that I am. As I continue to reflect back, I realize the challenges I was faced with were potential life takers – spiritually or physically. The fact that my mind was tormented and I was so broken inside, but yet I was still able to uphold the image as if I had no worries without breaking, speaks high volumes to the woman I am. Not to mention the lives I have touched along the way. And in such a broken state of being, people still looked up to me. This only shows me how much stronger and more effective I will be when I'm operating in total truth. God made no mistakes in making me – I just allowed the enemy to pervert the cause. However, at the end of the day, it will all be used for kingdom purposes.

The purpose of this letter is to inform my readers of how important it is to find your true identity. People die every day not knowing what their purpose is in life because they could not find their way back from life's detours. They lost their true self inside the person they created, which became their "truth," and they were not able to identify their authentic being that was always present but trapped in the lie.

Genesis 50:20
"But for you, you meant evil against me, but God meant it for good. What the devil meant for evil, God will turn it around for your good."

Special Thanks

THERE ARE A FEW people who deserve to be acknowledged. These people are key factors in who I am becoming. They all helped me in one way or another and motivated me when I needed it most. They let me know when I was right or wrong, and they all keep me lifted in their own individual, unique way.

My first thanks goes to my parents. Although I did not agree with a lot of things as a child, as an adult, I now understand. There are some things that I still do not agree with, but I understand it was all for a cause. My mother and I are very close, but we clash as well. I know it's because she wants the best for me, and at times it is hard for her to take off her mommy hat when she feels I'm heading for self-destruction of any sort. I love her because no matter how much I pushed her away, she was always there pulling me back. She is one of the purest women I know and she wears many hats in my life.

My father showed me the true meaning of love through the way he loved my mother and me. I put my father through very hard times growing up. I was filled up with all different sorts of anger, emotions, hurt, hatred, etc. and there were so many things I just didn't understand. I acted out all of these feelings, and my father got the worst of it. However, through it all, he NEVER turned his back on me. He was always there and made sure that I had the best of everything I needed. I will always love him for who he is.

My next thanks goes to Ms. Kim. She has always been there when I needed her. She plays a very significant part in my life and growth. I can always count on her to put me in my place. (Smiles)

Then we have my other mother, Mrs. Yvette Ellis. This woman is so dear to me. I love her honesty, and she holds no punches. She helps me stay in line and continuously reminds me of my purpose so I will never get far from it.

Mrs. Marion – I consider her my spiritual mother. Words cannot express my appreciation to her. She keeps me grounded in reality.

Aunt Rocky is one woman I can always count on to help

me figure out what I don't understand.

Schanell "Nellie" my baby cousin whom I love dearly! Thank you for being you and never switching up but always respecting my change. Let this book bless you.

My Nana. She doesn't say much, but when she does, I can expect a profound word. Her love is pure as gold.

Last but not least, Shayla Poindexter. As a teenager, this woman took care of me when I was in my worst stages of the streets, at an early age when I first ran out and began moving around recklessly. Her doors were always open to me. I mean she really looked out. She made sure I was good at all times. She let me know when I was moving too fast and when I needed to slow down. She is still someone that I know I can call when I need her, and she will be right there with no questions asked.

If I did not mention you directly, please do not charge it to my heart. I love and appreciate each and every one of you. (You know who you are.)

Dedication

I DEDICATE THIS BOOK to the memory of Jesse "Mook" Lanier. Jesse played a very important role in my life. There were some things that I did not understand until after he passed away and my lifestyle began to change. God used Jesse as a vessel to help change my life. A very important person once said to me, "Destiny, if you are going to be a part of Jesse's life and you want to see him live, you need to get yourself together and line up with the will of God." I never understood how my lifestyle could affect him, so it did not hit me where it should have.

One day, Jesse and I were lying in bed talking, and then somehow we fell asleep. When we woke up, he was on the edge of the bed and I was on his backside with my arm around him. As I went to move over, he grabbed my arm and said, "Don't move. You are right where I need you to be." Of course, I did not understand until he began to speak more. He said, "My life is on the edge. I don't have much time left. I need you to cover me. You don't have that much more time, but you have more time than me." I was speechless and did not say a word. The words that were spoken to me began to replay in my mind.

When Mook first passed away, I felt like I failed him. We were in a bad place, and I let my feelings disrupt the purpose, which allowed the enemy to come in and cause division. Jesse and I had been close friends since I was twelve and he was fourteen. We were from the same neighborhood and lived a street over from each other, so our relationship was beyond the typical girlfriend/boyfriend status. No matter what our title was, there would always be 100% unconditional pure love. So even on bad terms, the love still remained the same, and we both knew we could depend on each other no matter what.

On a separate occasion, Mook randomly woke up out of his sleep and said, "There is a war going on but you have to understand that the battle is not yours." It was so random that I did not know how to respond.

So I asked, "Why did you just wake up and say that?"

He said, "God told me to."

I understand that now more than ever. I have gone in so many circles fighting battles that are not mine to fight. The minute I gave it to God, the struggle was over, for he gives me strength and patience to endure. About two weeks before Mook passed away, he called me and said that he had been listening to this song and he thought about me every time he heard it, so he told me to listen to it. The song was "Be Blessed" by Yolonda Adams. Now every time I hear that song it touches my heart to the core, and it comes on at the right time and gives me the encouragement that I need. I really wish he were here. He is one of few friends that I did not ever have to question about his love. Mook would be so proud of my growth.

I decided to dedicate this book to the memory of Jesse "Mook" Lanier because he saw things inside of me before I was able to see them in myself. Jesse was always trying to bring out the best in me and was willing to invest in all that he saw. Mook was my partner in the life events that pushed me to change my lifestyle. He would be so proud to know that I am still maintaining the walk that we started together. He told me before I could even see that I would become this person that I am becoming today. I miss him so much! As I release more series, I will reveal more of our story from this chapter in my life.

Final Thoughts

AS I CONCLUDE THESE letters, I would like my readers to understand that it's an everyday struggle, but life is what you make it. Daily, we will be faced with temptations and obstacles. Just know that the battle is already won, so our duty is to position ourselves to manifest the victory. We have power over the enemy, and he preys on our weaknesses.

James 4:7
"Submit to God. Resist the devil and he will flee."

As people, we take scripture and utilize the parts that we find appealing and get partial results. That is because we leave out the groundwork of the scripture. Example: We focus toward resisting the devil and he will flee, and then we wonder why when we resist he does not flee. This is because we ignored the most important part of the passage and have not submitted ourselves to God. We have to make sure that our daily walk lines up with the word. However, we will fall sometimes, but that does not mean to stay down.

Romans 3:23
"For all have sinned and fall short
of the glory of God."

God knows what we are going to do before we even do it.

My life has been a consistent battle. Some times were harder than others, and I often felt like giving up. But that was not an option. I now thank God for the struggle because it made me who I am. Without the life experience, I could not effectively fulfill my purpose. I understand that a thief will not look in your window and rob an empty house. So if the enemy looked into your future and saw there was nothing there, he would move right past you because you don't have anything he wants. The greater the blessing, the harder the struggle. God gives his hardest battles to his strongest people, as he has to know that he can trust you when blessings start flowing. In my opinion, life's situations do not make or break you – they make you more of whom you really are.

1 Corinthians 10:13

"There isn't any temptation that you have expe-
rienced which is unusual for humans. God, who
faithfully keeps his promises, will not allow you to
be tempted beyond your power to resist. But when
you are tempted, he will also give you the ability
to endure the temptation as your way of escape."
(Gods Word Translation)

God will not put more on you than you can bear. So know that if he brings you to it, he will bring you through, and you are provided with all you need to overcome. My life is a living proof.

Let these letters bless your heart and ease your mind. Life is a gift so open up daily. More series to come.

Prayer

God, I just want to thank you for providing me the opportunity to reach out to your people through the writing of this book. I ask you to bless every individual who looks at this book, even if it's just to read the title and put it back down. Allow the title alone to minister to one's heart that they will begin a dissection. Lord, without you, none of this would be possible, and I am forever in debt to you. Thank you for my struggle, and more so for bringing me through when I thought I could not take any more. You showed up right on time. Lord, cover my readers and me as we continue this journey called life. Speak to my heart and direct my steps as you produce more series to serve your people.

Thank you, Amen.

"Self is the only prison that can bind the soul."
~ Henry van Dyke

To Be Continued...

About the Author

BORN AND RAISED IN Columbus, Ohio, Destiny Barrett had always been big-hearted and enthusiastic. But as the strains of life's many challenges took their toll, cracks started to form under that positive facade. Beneath her smiles lay nagging twangs of confusion and bitterness. *Trapped in the Lies of Your Truth* is Destiny's first foray into writing, and uncovers the importance of finding the truth of inner issues that are lost beneath external deception. The book draws from her experiences of taking wrong turns in life, clinging on to a sliver of hope, and eventually breaking out of the cycle of negativity. Not one to give up, Destiny obtained her high school diploma at the age of twenty-six, and went on to obtain a Diploma for Managing Cosmetology at twenty-eight years old. To Destiny, cosmetology has become more than a profession. In her day-to-day interaction with her clients, Destiny finds herself committed to providing a listening ear and offering a sister/mother-like refuge.

Drawn to youth issues, Destiny is a youth mentor, and prior to entering the cosmetology industry full-time, she worked with youths at a juvenile treatment facility for some six and a half years. Destiny enters into some of her most peaceful and creative moments while singing, making music and servicing her clients. She realized that God was preparing her for her Destiny even through the most struggling times in her life. By sharing her story of healing, Destiny hopes to inspire others to uncover their true hearts.